EMOTION INDUSTRY
TRACY DIMOND

BARRELHOUSE BOOKS

Published by Barrelhouse Books
Baltimore, Maryland
www.barrelhousemag.com

Published in the United States of America
ISBN 13: 979-8-9850089-2-0

First Edition
Cover art and book design by Shanna Compton

A thing grows into the light available to it.
This is not just a metaphor.

—*Rough Likeness: Essays*, Lia Purpura

Everybody's sick for something that they can find fascinating
Everyone but you and even you aren't feeling well

—"Astronaut," Amanda Palmer

CONTENTS

TODAY IS FIRE / TODAY IS FIRE / TODAY IS FIRE / TODAY
IS FIRE / TODAY IS

Step 1.

I'm looking for a system to buy into.
Raise the volume for paid programming.
How many special updates
until a broadcast becomes meaningless?

This may or may not be unsubstantiated:
I'm faking my death in time for the holidays.
People won't recognize me, but they will scream my name.
Time to admit—
I am terrified / I am ready.

Step 2.

Follow strict guidelines to transmit ideas.
The Internet is a case study of obsessions:

Everything has been claimed.
Everything has been published.
Everything has been resealed.

Step 3.

Instead of logging on,
I eat hardboiled eggs and marvel at the yellow yolks.
Will you take context seriously?
I'm not okay, I promise.
Smiling is an easy mask to wear.

Step 4.

My nerves mount around people who seem to cope.
It's the kind of day everyone else does it better.
It as in leaving the house.

Hairspray doesn't keep me in line.
Split ends don't cure themselves.
Baths cure my knots,
but paying for energy feels wasteful,
like live coverage of an empty ocean.
Direct mail catalogues are insidious
because each new pillow promises self-actualization.

Step 5.

I don't want to be told anything.
I want to feel the sun in my palms,
fingers stretched to the wind—

so I'm looking for a place with light,
windows that open,
and roof access because I like to tan
and pretend I live in the skyline.

I know exactly what I'm doing
So let me bottle the light in your eyes

VOMIT GLITTER / VOMIT GLITTER / VOMIT GLITTER / VOMIT

I dress as projection,
then dress for protection.

Upward mobility?
So bent over from this *leaning in*.
And my knees! Worn to the floor.

In a roomful of men, I'm told
I want your tan.

Trees look the same
until you notice their bend.
There is so much expanse because sky.

When clarity is the goal
I feel silvery gray,
like the concept of hair v. age.

Time did *this* to me.
Time can take *it* away.

WHAT ABOUT A BODY EXHIBIT / WHAT ABOUT A BODY EXHIBIT / WHAT ABOUT A BODY

I strive to fit an exhibit on special request. You'll watch me unpack groceries, drop a fresh dozen eggs, and receive age as a form of self-hate.

Sign up for reintegration to strip malls and chain restaurants to stop screaming: *treat yourself* really means *feel better about buying products that slowly kill you.*

Check out that face—looking to be noticed, but not noticed because those eyes are down. It takes one statement to start a spiral.

Buy instructions on mastering body, intimacy, and compromise. Now use memory. Can saving face protect you?

Picture a spectacle where expectation is out of place. If flawless is removing all controls, it's time reconsider moisturizer.

WHY DON'T YOU REST / WHY DON'T YOU REST / WHY DON'T YOU REST / WHY

Survey says: flawed methodology.

Send expectations to sunsets then institute a new fad: living as a social process.

Whatever—we are ticking. There's a landmine treaty America won't sign and I can't figure out these tax requirements.

Every day is work for feminists because hair is down / age is up. Every day is a party for feminists because hot pants are business.

Don't forget to pack a sweater to withstand chilling thoughts. Skin lasts more than nothing and I scream more when there are tangible days.

A woman speaking her mind is not entertainment. I just want to sync our cycles, then paint the town with period blood.

Break into the crime scene cleanup business to view emotion as industry.

NEW STANDARDS / NEW STANDARDS / NEW STANDARDS / NEW

Around source emotion I like to pretend I don't exist. Steroids don't cause depression. American paranoia causes depression.

Public posture: stably unstable. Is gas so expensive because nobody owns the water? Tell me: what is it like to be paid to gamble with other people's money.

Motorcyclists stop on the highway to watch the trees. People can open or break a heart. I'm no longer interested in irony.

Do you want it this way because you were raised? I'm worried about the men that remember my name. I find them useless as an infinity pool.

They'll love me if I stop questioning what they want. They'll love me if I'm the right condition. Question the muse: genius or hysterical?

Everything takes a stand. Everyone pays bills. We are all future and poised to take a human stance.

When I protect my hair
I don't protect my health
I only want you to pull my hair tonight

LOVE TAN / LOVE TAN / LOVE TAN / LOVE TAN / LOVE

I am romantic like the smell
of clothes draped in crime drama.
Don't pee in the water,
pee in the woods.

I have a crush on the world,
but it is not treating me well.
If I am an object, I am an
object of your nightmares.

Construction trucks stop in front of me,
then put up the LANE CLOSED sign.
How easily can you crack my spine
and find a way for our bones to touch?

Every poem is a love poem
in which we play a love game.
I want to feel all the tiny steps
of our tanned destruction.

Will you kiss each vertebrae?
We are *alone together*.

Let's just have a pillow fight party.
Hurt each other with feathers.

I am going to climb my loft bed
and kiss the spiderwebs.

GET OUT / GET OUT / GET OUT / GET OUT / GET
after Clifton Gachagua

DJ, think about our songs in the 21st century.
Say, *don't hate the player, hate yourself*
because that's a definable state.

Dating rocks is a complex process. So is dating rockers.
It's okay, I'll keep using my credit card
until the academy updates the system.

Scientists report that increasing skirt size
increases the risk of breast cancer.
And you thought poets didn't make sense.

There is this myth about noble hobbies
with which I disagree. Art isn't for looks.
If you want to be a mermaid, buy a mermaid tail.

I always remember coffee, but breakfast is so hard.
Aging is deciding which system to buy into,
but I'm still searching for shooting stars.

I can't see constellations through clouds and smog,
though a tar roof feels like sand under socks.
Sometimes it's nice to sit outside and not be seen.

I don't think violence will fix anything.
No daisies grow from my anus, but I still believe in sun and I'm looking for a way to invite you in.

A GIRL CAN CHANGE THE WORLD WITH A BEDAZZLER

Think about the times
you speak of sparkles

over the times
you watch *Meet the Press.*

Divide that by
the accountants that read fiction,

articles documenting the use of YOLO
after a cancer diagnosis.

Bodies leaving the house
consume each other.

I'm going to die
and it's not from the stains.

Unicorns weep in my hair,
my bed is stripped of comfort.

AFTER RILKE

I recommend
zero percent
of my attitudes.

No, I don't think
this string of bad luck
came from a chain letter
I didn't send in 1999.

Your schedule will kill you
if you don't calendar some fun,
so wander Whole Foods
like you can afford $12 granola.

Please, my organic look
is questioned
when I wear neon purple
to a fracking protest.

Why must I change my life?
I have only a few years
until scoliosis gets my posture.

AN ABRIDGED MEDICAL HISTORY

When I think of my body
I think *whateves*.
Fifty percent of humans have bulging discs,
but what will you say when
I tell you my mom was exposed to DDT?
My brother and I are
androgynous mirror images.

Why would anyone use my face
as an example of kindness?
If my behavior is unsatisfactory,
prescribe a serotonin balance
illustrated with clouds and sunlight.

Do you think back pain is in my head?
I don't want to sit, stand, or lie.
Here's a clear diagnosis:
My doctor said *awesome*
when I felt pain to the touch.

YOU DIDN'T CHOOSE / YOU DIDN'T CHOOSE / YOU

The child's smile post hand transplant is more genuine than any I could know. It is easier to take in a tragic story than think about changing. We are seasoned enough in health to mourn the loss of innocence. Night and day hold the same secrets.

The verbs are chosen. You can cover up, but you still have a body you did not choose. Have you asked a problem-posing question yet? It's not yes or no, but what or why. Human coverage. Oh, too human.

Follow a healthcare infomercial with a flawless makeup commercial. Message: treat a shell and move on. Remember protecting an egg as a school exercise? Do it 24/7 as an adult.

The egg is your heart. When someone says you are not possible, remember to look. The collective *we* follows.

Alone on the dance floor in Atlantic City, a man cries for a pity dance. I run to my friends to tell them I was right: you cannot be alone as a woman in public. Take a class to explain incorrect categorization.

When you make me feel unsafe, I want to make you feel how I feel—skin pulling off your eyes, never able to look behind you fast enough, every noise someone with a knife because you *look* like easy prey.

Of course I want to be a brand. Then I would have some rights. If everything is irony, I wouldn't feel the gerbils pawing through my chest. That attempt to quote a mid-twentieth-century advertisement—a flat sound.

Attention is the question. Moan *howl at the moon*, but did you forget already? The moon glows in daylight too. Fight for sound in a tunnel of sheets, fight for sound when people stare you to pieces.

I WATCH DOCUMENTARIES INSTEAD OF HORROR FILMS

When I'm bored with horror films
I remember that the top scientists
are researching cellulite causes.

Why doesn't age have a leash?
I believe enriched cereal
will enhance my bra size.

Synapses are a firing squad
while we're losing the battle
against underarms.

My diagnosis was to relax.
If you put your tongue on my spine
I would feel some calm.

I don't think I deserve
any more free samples.

ATTEMPT TO DEFINE REALITY / ATTEMPT TO DEFINE

Self-portrait as a collage of Francis Bacon paintings
        because LOL @ realism,

Self-portrait under headphones
        listening to emo rock while
        falling into teenage waterfall of emotions
        in lines from you sent back to you
        as I renounce capitalism
        and a new pop star is born—

        Then every moment I wear prescription
        sunglasses trying to look my age.

        The definition of age subsists in saved
        calendars.

Whatever!

Self-portrait:
        every time I look in a mirror,
        every time I agonize over lipstick,
        every time a television commercial sends me
to Amazon,

every time I watch you watch me,
every time I Google bipolar disorder
because I'm paranoid that depression
isn't *just* depression.

Oh my God!

A self-portrait where you can renounce your words
and hold the cognitive dissonance in your heart.

I stand at warrior one touching one more phantom limb left in
strands on the operating table.

I'm stable, I'm stable—
can't you see me hold this pose?

Self-portrait offended the moment I was told
I looked *like a blush wine drinke*r, as if long hair and
light makeup is behavior disrobed.

Take it easy, light brown hair girl-next-door
reading Steinbeck in the backyard.
Could someone *please* tell me
how young I look again?

Again!

Self-portrait four Sierra Nevadas into the night thinking about
the body—

>the reign of terror over every moment captured in
>store mirrors that are free promotion for pop
>culture's reflection.

Always acting like no one is watching—
Did you know one day you would eat razors and time?

A picture lasts so long!

Self-portrait uncontained in my body: dye my hair, contour
my face,

>never turn the computer off.
>when I ask, *are stars just like me?*
>say *they buy groceries and have anxiety.*

Anyway, all the billboards are about God
or plastic surgery.

Self-portrait stating *I am* felt like a good idea once.

Take off your belt and your shirt and your bra,

>I heard it means you side with freedom.
>But do I really want to give you that much?

A real self-portrait nests in a naked body suit
of written flaws exposing the other
self-portrait on Halloween

I'll say it to your face and I'll say it from rooftops:
everything is reality.

Surprise!

A body identity I touch is the privilege of
a bag of muscles and bones and fat
with a voice box.

Does this make you hate me a little?
That's acknowledging worth.
I am the terror you feel
when you realize credibility is a construct.

Advice for identity from an outside source:
Stay stubborn now.
Never be stopped.

If the temperature keeps rising,
Oceans will turn into liquid dead zones
The march to disaster needs a positive playlist

EVER HEARD OF THIRD EYE BLIND?

Tonight, I am Googling
the term: *sincere orgasm*
after my sixth Bud Light Lime.

Think about the times you karaoke
to Third Eye Blind
wanting to relive your first love.
90s rock is best
for masturbation.

It equals the times
you look at band tattoos
and try not to shout: *overstatement.*
Spend infinity looking for something else
that appeals to multiple generations.

The ocean is the only thing
I can talk back at
when I'm in a crop top.
Don't think about geography
while plugged into iPod magic.

AFTER POP MUSIC

I whisper while cooking:
hot and dangerous.
I have hot pants on
because it's 90 degrees.

I pull slacks over my tan.
I'm aware of the stares
but *plenty of people
looked queerer than I*.

Dear starving artist,
I'll pay for your snack.
You owe me a beer
and a hand job.

In the halls of the library
I write in the margins:
suck my dick.

I'm going to die
from all this mental labor.

MOMENTUM

I've been thinking about self-actualization
since I stripped to my underwear
for beer at the gay pride parade.
My cooking montage feels
more serious since downloading
Wu-Tang Clan. Philosophy isn't summarized
in a trainer's tagline, but more people
should join a gym
for the complimentary coffee.

I'm worried about how the next generation
will handle the apocalypse.
Not running from zombies
as they complain about pool blisters,
but who will scream from rooftops
if they're searching for air-conditioned rooms?

I gather fireflies
And keep them in a drawer
For something to follow

CLEARVIEW MANOR

Tell me salvation
is ten colonial homes away.

I am a traffic sign
in my neon dress.

My intersection is stranger
to the sky.

Reconstruct memories
with new road maps.

Rocks move for cement
swimming pools.

Cornfields bow
to suburban planning.

ARE YOU SATISFIED?

A marine biologist said:
manatees are slow-moving animals
without a hint of irony.

I want a song to summarize
philosophy of intention
in less than three chords.

Separate lights and darks
to organize a spectrum.
I kept laughing when I drew infinity.

If God loves ugly
I finally understand my childhood.

If I could put out fires with gasoline
I would be a well-done ocean heart.

STARTUP

Change the world
without stepping outside.

Find a moment
to upload empathy,

post a status supporting
a self-esteem campaign.

Admit bullying
weeds out the weak:

real estate prices
remain manageable.

FIVE YEARS

Time sucks fruit dry
while radio hits stay sweet.

I transcend teenage angst
reading DNA on my smartphone.

I try to be nicer
to the human mirror.

I want to teach children to read
with the lines on my face.

Don't get old is uttered by someone
touting the value of tube socks.

Left alone for five years,
I'm not stale yet.

I CHASE ENDINGS

I turn on good-looking news
in time to burn my morning coffee.

I move my car into the tow zone
to get more notes in the mail.

Then you ask if I want kids
like I can pick them at a kennel.

My bones speak with nerve endings,
while you chase vocabulary away.

Funnel retirement funds
through the spinal investment channel.

Beige walls wash out my mind,
I want to paint billboards purple.

Say it's not my fault that
my angels recite pharmaceutical scripts.

BUT YOU DON'T WANT ME

Tomorrow will be such a nude morning
I mean nice.

I want to buy an RV,
I want to kiss each time zone.

Did you know
Yellowstone is a giant volcano?

I'm falling over
the age of rocks.

I thought I was sick
But the thermometer said
To get a deeper tan

PUKING AMERICAN DREAMS

Under my insurance deductible,
excitement is discouraged.

It gets all judgmental
when I phone in for sequins.

I am a brand
reflecting stage lights.

My platinum perfected
before cancer treatments,

my voice engineered
with auto-tuned emotion.

I am easier to swallow
than a morning dose of General Mills.

I GOT SO SAD

Rule number one
is cardio.

I can outrun anxiety
with the newest-model shoe.

I know I am an age,
but I should believe

puppies live forever at the end of rainbows
and my vote matters.

I keep trying to return my body
but could not get anyone

to pay the shipping on eBay.
If magazines are so good

at calculating calorie deficits
why don't they manage the economy?

I lighten the ends of my hair
to pretend sunshine flows through me.

Take time to hide or reveal in the daily art of getting ready. There is a type of landslide called, for its movement and personality. I feel a kinship to nature.

Strip down to show nothing, then curl my hair because downward spiral. Highlights are planned effervescence. Your choices are validated by likes.

Happiness exists in the morning. It wanes in the afternoon with my self-control. Whatever—tans should be rationed for free. To find sun, I climb trees that weep.

These tattoo guns are hard to wield, but how else will we remember names? When asked why anyone would practice self-destruction, soil says *it's only a test.*

What else scares you? Try to find some gravity. The best advice I've heard lately? *Run while you can.*

FAVORITE

I know you are my favorite product
when I look in your face.

Good luck fighting your timeline,
the nicest storefronts are funeral homes.

Products will be bought online
while we wage a war against age.

I would feel settled
if you put your tongue in my spine.

Living forever
is reason to procrastinate.

For best results,
forget about gravity.

WHY THESE BONES / WHY THESE BONES WHY THESE BONES / WHY THESE

Keep writing lists, keep smelling for hair. Television networks report: *there was this place that felt like identity, but it was only a memory.*

I've never feared drowning, but recognize the crushing tide. Don't romanticize ruin. Even in its uncertainty, this is a journey metaphor.

Will you perform for the moon's rays tonight? Disregard horoscopes. Someone must understand that no one is fit for human interaction.

I'm not talking about positives developments. I'm talking about modification for defense. Time doesn't tick at the same rate of gravity. Everyone should laugh at time. I keep a file for possible nose jobs.

Is self-loathing sitting under the sun like an underwatered flower? I'm walking in silence, but strangers want to know what I'm doing after work.

I'm silent because screaming causes a scene. Then discover he's whispering in my ear: *I'll find you again when no one is watching.*

SEND THE WHITE FLAG / HA / NO / HA / NO / HA / NO /
HA / NO / HA / NO / HA

There is a concern that poems
are not logical sequences
like neutral proofs.
Look at organisms that fake banality:
Sliced bread is not a neutral
benchmark for greatness.
Cells divided long before blades
were added to the equation.
Flowers are not neutral.
They open for the sun and fart oxygen.
Eating almonds while drinking
almond milk is not neutral.
It may be a form of cannibalism.

> Are you a pile of organic mush?

Bodies are not neutral.
PH is only neutral
if it is in balance.
Colors are not neutral,
everyone has a emotion painted into a hue.
Their can be neutral,
but sexuality is not neutral.

How about heterosexuals come out
before I have to say anything.
This tan is not neutral; I've spent years with it.
Where are my crow's feet?
Age is not neutral.
It contains perceived credibility.

     Wait.

Open space is owned by someone
or something.
Corporations are not neutral
they have charters
then develop office policies
and insurance programs
that change your behavior.
Diet Coke is not neutral
when it slides down your throat
or sits next to Pepsi.
Loving you less is neutral
when you're already looking ahead.

     Take a look at embedded assumptions.

The net is not neutral.
Activity is not neutral.
Activism is not neutral.

Every activist takes responsibility
stopping and making traffic.
They help us see.
Memory is not neutral.
History is even less neutral,
which is clear in biography,
but even more clear in autobiography.

Which story prompts your day?

Getting into a car is not neutral
when it's an order.
Survey the people that force it every day,
then force yourself to get dressed.
An outfit is never neutral.
My performance is not neutral.
Watch the weird thoughts in your head.

If I could purchase time
I would leave Tracy to pay the rent,
And survive on water and sunshine

REMEMBER TO LOOK YOUNG / REMEMBER TO LOOK / LOOK

Call it art,
but 100 percent of exes say
they can't get close to me.

What does that mean?
Each has been introduced
to the front-clasp bra.

Why should we talk
about feelings openly?
I'm all memories.

Everyone wants
to be so nice,
but I want to accomplish.

Fill out the survey:
your feedback is valued
when proposing a threesome.

Then remember how to look young:
lay me by the pool
and soak my hair in bleach.

UNIVERSAL TRUTHS

When I say it's going to be sunny,
I'm only being real.
Substitute bagel for angel
and you have heaven on Earth.

My carb to tweet ratio
is off the charts.
No one says *I love cancer*,
but sunlight is fantastic.

I found natural glow sticks
in the summer.
Time to paint the world
with firefly smears.

Time to share:
making someone food says
I like you enough
to want you alive.

APPLY FOR THE ROLE / APPLY FOR THE ROLE / APPLY

To whom it may concern,
are emotions an industry?

I am a revolutionary project.
Apply a beauty patch
and control my mind.

        Five minute hair,
        five minute identity.

Do you like my old soul?
I am not smiling for your
pink pharmaceuticals.

But I'm so fresh—

        Eating toothpaste,
        chugging mouthwash.

I'm approaching an age
where getting it together
is a war on authenticity.

Every day feels like
a weapon of mass destruction
marketed for the 11 o'clock news.

LANDSCAPE / LANDSCAPE / LAND ESCAPE

What if there were budget cuts to oxygen? We are
bags of energy until our motivation runs out. The
weather forecast is a daily alarm, so what I did I do
to deserve YouTube commercials about retirement
plans? Privilege is not worrying every time you go
outside.

Even online is outside. Do not read the comments.
When a child says *I could do that* in response to art,
say *you should do it*. Tolls are nothing like a tax on
the heart: $22.15 I still want to see you. Show this
feeling: waiting for someone to die.

There is an evolution of why and how in every
day. Changed my approach from what is right to
what is potential. Use animal instincts listening for
footfalls and wheels. Define the cost in progress.

You are alive until you are dead. No, I am not
special, I am trying to be less depressed. A billboard
screams: *go outside and live!* Thank you for the
feedback. Waking is it, the rest is up to you.

Distribute resources. Are you looking for proof?
Forget landscape paintings as clear reality. Birds
scream in the wind. They feel what is next.

COSMIC ELECTRIC TIME / COSMIC TIME / COSMETIC

What if the rainbows in my hair
found a path through the cosmos to you?
Will we move to the ocean for a love affair,
the sandcastles home until the tide breaks?

Do you manifest destiny
through personal relationships?
What war are we still in?
Do you wonder if we have colonized our hearts?

Why do we still have daylight savings time—
can't we have double summertime?
When will poetry wear the tan of professional wrestling?
Maybe tans build bulk around the canon?

How will my mind stop chanting
when will *so close* mean touching
on a rooftop, telling the stars they can only
be as human as our questions?

The space and time we inhabit is vital. I checked my watch. I just checked my watch. I didn't countdown on NYE. My resolutions care too much about time. Your two cents ring like an empty water glass.

No, this is not an answer. The car started and we are wearing [freedom]. If I move my hand an inch your coat electrifies my being. No again. Your coat sets my teeth on edge. This time is sundown and nothing is proven.

There was some debate last night. Right. There was. I fucking hate passive voice. Each blade cuts water as I remember your hairline. Your blue eyes. Your expectation. Split the check. Time asked for groceries in the bending light.

Those expectations again. A woman's narrative. The human narrative. From behind what is the difference. I'm going to write these words on shower curtains in bike lanes in holy holes because Ginsberg forgot about a lot of us. I am sorry, he affected me so much at nineteen. The effects are not gone.

I don't have eight hours I have fifteen minutes under a statue and people still push me out early so they can consume the art. Look up and lose thought. See—the sun is warm anyway. This process is edits but sometimes I need raw emptiness to know the moon is full.

My hands still aren't steady but I think Fiona Apple has covered that topic. Milk continues to spill but I do not buy it—I drop eggs again. Expect these words to never stop.

I am a statue with her arms full of glory. I is not me but a moment of thought. Philosophy did not bring this. Time brought this. Have you seen *A Christmas Carol?* "You fear the world too much." That's all I remember before falling asleep.

People ask where poems come from and *I say I let them become then I edit a new reality.* Forget raw material. I've used no many times on purpose. I admit when giving my number is a mistake. Alison left every journal blank. I [would] say I care about objects, not words, but I visit museums to read the words.

I'm really hungry. That's not a metaphor. Simple statements knife the conscious. *I'm a nice guy.* Instead, I say things to myself like *I'm going to make grapefruit.* What's it like to have a regular-sized fridge? I could be a bigger person, but I'd rather ignore you.

FISCAL FALLOUT

The Republican Party
is more popular than the Kardashians
but less popular than cockroaches.

I'm building a team
out of local weathermen.
Who's to say what's obscene?

We must prepare—
whiten our teeth,
swallow bleach.

Our infertility
riding the tides
is the perfect constituent.

If we experience a fallout,
I'll sequester your bones
for the perfect broth.

GIVE ANSWERS / GIVE ANSWERS / GIVE ANSWERS / GIVE

Squat over holes
and call it protest.
Then smile because
that's what everyone says to do.

Art crisis, send existential help:
dress the trees with toilet paper
because our adolescent understanding
never evolved past the sun.

Turn off your savior complex.
I don't know a plainer way
to say how I feel.

Let's argue the weather,
glitter, the purpose of sex.
Unwrite the rules of femininity.
Unwrite the tidiness.

Undo because look at today.
Turn off the default setting.
This body is burning and still aging.

CONSTRUCT / CONSTRUCT / CONSTRUCT

Blush wine does not equal boring. Let's ask
questions first, like what is the energy in bones and
how can we explain future tans?

Gender is fluid and your hair looks good tonight.
I'm still painting my nails because all my friends
left to have sex together.

I'm waiting for time, the mail, and a banner behind
a commercial jet. Thanks for the note—I wouldn't
date me either.

Hands have a grip, so we can talk about moon
phases now. If there is no response, remember that
blisters on a heart are hard to clean.

Are skinned knees worth participation? Take raw
knuckles as art. I'm hanging on to a one percent
when I'm ninety-nine percent sure nothing matters.

If things are going to get better, we have to start
using our perfect teeth.

I'd like to be an organ donor
Give away my eyes,
Then I can watch the world
Without replacing my shoes

RESIST DANCE / RESISTANCE

Why is there resistance to improvement?
You should want to strive
I changed a light bulb within twelve hours,
you could say I'm pretty successful
My dad showed me he has a free pass to national parks as a senior
I have a future to strive for
but I don't know how to put my shoulders back

When I see couples I'm like
oh nice you get to have sex often with someone you definitely like
I have nightmares when I'm excited
A bad potato is easier to identify than a bad egg
Like, that cliché is so true
Is this the right time to talk
about Plan B as the most honest drug results?
Proof of effectiveness is on the packaging:
You'll know it works when you are not pregnant

It would be more useful for me to consistently go to the doctor
    than the gym
Some days, you must choose between a deluxe bank or a deluxe gym
In other words, how do you show your status?
It's easier to use resistance bands than resist the patriarchy
I am not trying to be irreverent

Ever analyze the arch in your foot?
Language is weird to me, so is land
and the bodily obsession with our gravitational pull
Our weight is our pull towards each other
We are so obsessed with identifying difference
That goes right into the statement:
Those with money dictate the rules
and I am ruled by what I hear

It's that feeling when you hear rumors about yourself and think *true*
Can you tell I am working on my moxie?
A major author identified me as
the young person with the microphone

I also wrote a book called *Sorry I Wrote So Many Sad Poems Today*
Now strangers want to tell me what to write
There is no comment card on my book,
but you can write about it on your blog, or better yet,
please write a review for a major publication
We cannot touch our idols, but they teach us

Body confidence is walking into traffic without looking both ways. Scream threats from background music: *Hope I don't lose it tonight.*

Have these websites found the landmine in my data? Advertisements are art if I'm your hobby. A nervous laugh relaxes furrowed brows.

Be an inspiration crying to the tides. Stroke my leg and tell me tattoos are the clearest scars. Nothing really matters if I'm frustrated with everyone equally.

He tolerated small talk, but I was out of condoms. He held my waist and said *I know you're doing this for the looks.*

Can I plant synthetic trees every place I wanted to be anonymous? I'm waiting for a second wind, so I feel my bones belong to me.

WHY DON'T YOU GET A REAL JOB / WHY DON'T YOU / WHY

My wrinkled shirt
doesn't wear heels.

I could stand out with a tan,
lecturing on the purpose of idioms.

What is the point of a ripe lemon?
I'm clutching library books

once pristine, now dog-eared
on feminist passages.

Changes are happening:
Look at daffodils that grow around highways.

I'm working hard!
Man-hours under the sun.

REAL LIFE LISA FRANK

I read that writing today lacks feeling.
Add that to the pile of laundry.

If I add rainbows to my hair
I might feel more range.

I started to look on the bright side
when I stopped getting paychecks.

Let's go to the dog park
and drink 40s in the trees.

I'm a baseball fan
now that I can paint my body orange.

Instead of oil
my power source is sweet potatoes.

I'm so high-functioning
it's time to buy a sectional.

I WANT FRANCIS BACON TO DRAW ME

I dream about a new blender
because mine screams

about a lack of channels
every time I floss.

If no one hears the fire alarm
is a tree falling in the woods?

A dash of acid to my face
will answer this question:

Would you still like my poems
if you didn't want to have sex with me?

Put my mind to canvas,
work my bones like rotted wood.

I'm trying to feel as strongly
as an exclamation point.

Do you want capitalist pleasures
Or capitalist rules?

DIE RHYMES WITH DIE

I heard a man say
that I do it for attention
I never thought of that
but now that you mention:

Dyed my hair to match my soul
has better reception than
dyed my hair to match my period.
How's that for a new blood metaphor?

Meg said I looked cool yesterday.
I feel like I've achieved something.
Was that a Facebook status or an acceptance speech?
Pay attention to me.

What is looking like a woman?
Try to eradicate that paranoid state.
I'll have a kale salad with kale.
Yes, I am a feminist still trying to be a size.
This is the forum of public opinion, right?

I'm going to say to the next person
that tells me to smile:
I hope the world makes you feel how I feel.

Does the earth apologize for taking up space?
This is getting dark, but in a tasteful way.
Someone on *Meet the Press*
said we're in a *post-truth election*.

REPLY ALL to the world:
has groupthink caught you?
Health is behavior disrobed, so take it easy—
the best part of being human
is putting on clean underwear.

If you're six times more likely to die on a plane than train, when will our planet sigh at the weight we create? The minute you say hip, you are focusing too much on how people perceive you. The news has become a cycle of letting everyone know news will come.

No one talks to men about having the face for short hair. *I will not take the bait, I will not take the bait, I will not take the bait.* Thank god the old white man corrected me. Maybe more stores should sell positive attitudes.

The wildflowers are sponsored by the days you look for your heart. I know you have a script, but can you deviate and listen? Can't wait to be old enough that people don't think it's cute I do things. Just feeling lost so I'm reading my horoscope.

If fire will end suffering, I will ignite. Are you still thinking about the flowers? They coat your fingers with protection.

BLOOD PRESSURE WILL SQUEEZE YOU

What's the difference
between boredom and ADD?
Last summer's uplifting athlete
is this winter's murderer.

Is cable better
than a well-done steak?
I never order gifts
from infomercials.

I wrote to Hallmark:
Can a heart have a place?
The minimum emotional tax
comes directly to my door.

The doctor said:
you're diluting content.
What if I thin my blood
with bottled water?

A BRIEF HISTORY OF MEDICINE

How should doctors test
the new wave of pharmaceuticals?
We're lifers until the end.

If science was easy,
we would go back to 1871
when half the Harvard medical students
could read.

They hung bodies from the ceiling
to straighten spines.
When a diagnosis looks tough,
shake heads.

Mice exposed to GMOs
are infertile in a few generations.
Soon we'll have nothing to worry about.

I am working on a philosophy in which everyone says
Let's just make this bearable, ok?

WHAT'S A BODY

I started a war on billboards
but the resources in my emotional
hedge fund need consultation.
Make me a roadblock
on the George Washington Bridge.

Can't talk now, this
21st annual New Home Sale
has me mouthing
Webster's Dictionary online:
mechanical smiles.

Do straight-edgers get more done
in the war on drugs?
Does anyone care about
this war on apathy?

Every morning is
a post-coffee morning
filled with breaking news about
the next maple-syrup apocalypse.

Nest in my data of human behavior.
I was afraid of being found out—
until I realized
everything is performance.

Be a blank slate or explosion of identity. Don't apologize for the inconvenience. Follow the road signs to hell, but stop to read the insurance bills.

In parking lots we find place. The older we get, the harder it is to escape history. Let's explain who we are and why expectations are crushing.

We can't clean ourselves with bleach though the stink is under our nails. It would be easier to fuck the men that smile at me. Example: I said *no* and he said *but he bought me dinner.*

You know what they say about politics: change takes money. Business casual isn't the only avenue for respect. Apply to work at a strip club. Be paid for a body.

What if we all revealed our under-secrets? Look out for opportunity and purpose. Survival is an ambivalent concept.

Reach into your pocket and pull out a sun. Wake for the morning vomit routine. Keep following the line of syntax. *We get to do this, we get to do this, we get to do this.* If you have a question, Windex works on anything. I heard it on the *Today Show*. One time, a local news anchor asked me for a comment. I said I knew nothing about the trees. She asked again, *I just need a comment.*

Stick to your lies. They fill the holes in your ribs. Please help through this idea hangover prompted by *he hates me, he hates me more*. Stare into art as you wander a museum. A girl statue has her shoulders back and chin up. So gorgeous and full of male gaze. Is this where fears are made? Take responsibility stopping and making art.

Try to push your feet into your sternum. Dig into your heart. Existence is a metaphor for something. A couple I followed keeps looking back. It was nice they held the door. We must have the same goals, like, I also want a tender moment in the park. There is no more blending in, just leaves in my hair waves.

No one listens closely to the whispers, but the wind is changing and roots are crying for caress. Not putting a controlling hand on a shoulder, but an intertwining. Leaves continue as camouflage like the business casual in my closet. In long hair we trust. Ponytails will get work done because tans are fading like art in front of a window.

I paint my nails hot pink. It's *Fuchsia Power,* so I know that feminine display has a name. Now I feel like I joined the crowd. The state of a manicure is a sign of existential motivation. If you want to turn back choices, go to the basement so time will tick at a slower rate.

Invest in technology, then remember that the most accurate clock uses tinfoil. Maybe keep that stuff off your head. Time is a measure of chaos. A body is a measure of health. Take care of both: don't exit your car quickly at a gas station because you can set yourself on fire.

Don't show your hand. If you are a student, you should get a student ID for the discounts. You won't have them again until you are old enough to be sincere without undercutting irony. Remember that everyone has to clean their home.

Will you let go of control when approaching nature? Pansies bloom while lingering over a first love. Hearts hold, but I should have known it wasn't going to work when I said *I just want to be happy* and he replied *that's not something you can want.*

Clouds move past the moon on a long walk home. It feels like cheating to walk less than three blocks to an apartment. I'm not looking to be handed entrance. Every time I go outside I think *taking out the trash.*

Nervous laughter puts others at ease. Seek the value in hard work. Bleach hair to emphasize light. Buy teeth whitener to emphasize snarl. Look into the terror when you realize credibility is a construct. Follow wires.

SEARCH TERMS

I'm conducting research
on single poets
conducting research.

Selfies are moderated
versions of the ego.
They treat a lifelong
condition: emotions.

The NSA wastes time on my terms.
This might be forward,
but the weekly newsletter calls
for transparent windows.

Today, I'm going to U-turn
in the driveway
of the most beautiful house
in America.

Now, think about this weapon
of mass destruction:
the military has more funding than education.

REMEMBER FIRE / REMEMBER FIRE / REMEMBER FIRE / REMEMBER

When I was a kid, I thought all soup came from cans. Produce grew in stores, except for the carefully planted tomatoes in the backyard. Those stood until it was time for my brother and me to dig for grubs. To commit a capital offense in the home was to put away wet dishes. Dirt wasn't an issue. We always removed our shoes.

One day I overheard *the bigger the diamond, the bigger the divor*ce. I'll never get married. Not when it's happier to trust that someone will come back. We have too much perspective to romanticize pain. I hang to memories so I feel this is true, then I redefine excitement. For example, when my safety is commended I say *I'm not paying for an abortion.*

Take on new rules. Live on an edge. Drink water over a computer on a moving bus. Or leave a thank you card with your phone number in a public restroom. Tune the weather to traveler info then ask how you can get further away. Lifestyle moves everyone to use credit cards. Buy things to fit into the system. This abstraction builds on abstraction.

These wars look like movies, but we are not movie stars. Thinking takes so much time. If I have to confront the future, I think I figured out what to do while living in economic uncertainty. My five-year-plan is to not get hit by a car. My twenty-year-plan is to stay the same size so I don't need to buy new clothes when everything in my closet becomes vintage.

Yesterday a man yelled at me from his car. He said he wanted to ask to go where I was going. He said he didn't want me to feel weird, so he refrained. Living with a female body is political bargaining. A stroller abandoned on a highway makes more sense. It's a sense of going. Where do our warning labels go? Walking outside is a statement for these bodies connected to brains. Without bodies, brains don't have hands.

I remember I am more than a body when I am on the Internet. Text fills the situation. Well-chosen avatars create the context. A background can be a favorite thing. Do you confuse gender and performance? The correlation exists in hair and color. Today is fire. Sun in the eyes blocks out everything. I've finally made my peace as far as me and me go.

If there is no Internet after death,
Are affirmations stored in bones?

IN WHICH RESOLVE IS MADE TO ACT

Take on some inner peace.
Uninstall three applications today.

Shake in bones after two catcalls.
Their thoughts shape your route.

Travel through the minds of strangers.
Experience living in a body.

When in public, I am not public property.
The winter chills every new pair of slacks.

There is something else I should be doing.
This résumé won't update itself.

Perform the actions of creation.
Find fire in the heart of my computer.

What else could I want?
Birthday sex is one of my greatest accomplishments.

There is a fear of gradient that shades memory.
The ball has dropped on making nice.

I'm going to wear leggings
until strangers stop saying *be careful out there.*

I WATCH LOCAL TELEVISION FOR THE COMEDY

When did local news get heavy?
Let's chat about the moon
and it's flattering angles
on a sinking cruise ship.

I redefine danger
when I corral dolphins.
I use tulle to build a halo
around an endangered coral reef.

I read all the books
and still don't know
how to get game.
I'm looking for authenticity
in yearly subscriptions.

Why doesn't age have a leash?
I collect vitamin D
and worry age will betray me.

DID YOU COVER UP / DID YOU COVER UP / DID YOU COVER UP / DID YOU COVER

You can't pretend to be an animal for long. Soak in the sun, buried. Interrogate progress assumed in time. Interrogate dreams.

A costume is no attachment to identity. It's the impact of a different wardrobe. Youth in infinity defined by tan lines.

It's all fun and games until it's time to go outside. I don't want to hear the natural sounds of men hollering at me.

A summer wardrobe is ready for the sun like the neutral tide. Do you know how to talk about femininity divorced from fuckability?

I paint my nails and think gel is enough to *keep it together*. Propose a five vice limit. Listen to knees and lips tell a story.

I pull out my passport. Take me somewhere with this—burn my Social Security card and repaint my face. I chop off my unicorn hair in the new year.

SELF DIAGNOSIS

This manuscript is sponsored by
the fear that we may not be enough.

I'm getting spam for Senior Dating
because of the ailments I google.

I look for age at a discount
in the seafood section at Whole Foods.

I huff the hair in front of me,
it's a botanical garden.

Time for one-night stands in an unlocked car.
They aren't about me anyway.

One day I'll catch someone
setting up a highway memorial.

If laughter is the best medicine
I still can't catch my breath
when I look at the moon.

NOTES

p. 10 from "I'm Not Okay (I Promise)" by My Chemical Romance.

p. 13 yes, I did read *Lean In* by Sheryl Sandberg.

p. 14 a friend shared this squirrel fact.

p. 16 these motorcyclists stopped my heart in 2014.

p. 18 the truck did stop in front of me on the way to the library while listening to Fall Out Boy.

p.24 he said *awesome* while I wondered what my life would be like with scoliosis.

p. 26 many grimy beach bars are called Howl at the Moon.

p. 33 "talk back at the ocean" is a line from Third Eye Blind's "10 Days Late."

p. 34 lines from Kesha's "We Are Who We R" and Sylvia Plath's *The Bell Jar*, respectively.

p. 38 overheard on NBC's *The More You Know* in 2013.

p. 40 people are obsessed with telling the young to stay young.

p. 44 poem title from Marina and the Diamond's "Hollywood."

p. 48 end lines uttered to me on a lunch break in downtown Baltimore in 2012.

p. 57 the billboard spoke to me in 2016.

p .62 quoting 2013 *New Yorker* article.

p. 68 from Nicki Minaj and Cassie, "The Boys"

p. 73 epigraph quoting the Billy Talent (Pezz) song "M&M."

p. 76 yes, I'm referencing Oscar Pistorius.

p. 91 a common goodbye in Baltimore.

ACKNOWLEDGMENTS

Thank you to the following journals, websites, and blogs that have featured versions of these poems in a variety of forms: *Fact-Simile, Baltimore Style, Barrelhouse, Powder Keg, Truck* blog, *Dusie, The Nervous Breakdown, Pinwheel, similar:peaks::, Shabby Doll House, Sink Review, Coconut, Electric Cereal, glitterMOB, Weave Magazine, Seltzer Zine, Hidden City Quarterly, Everyday Genius, Haircut Genius, Super Awesome Mega Gigantic Pretty Sweet Friend Zine, apt, Ghost Proposal, Hobart, UP, Illuminati Girl Gang.*

Books could not exist without the support surrounding them. Thank you to the Barrelhouse team for your enthusiasm and support. Massive additional gratitude to:

The creative warmth of the Healthies: Tonee Mae Moll, Tyler Mendelsohn, Andrew Klein, mychael zulauf, Mandy May.

Amanda McCormick, for your years of friendship and creative collaboration. All the Ink Press Productions authors for their inspiration over the years.

The friends and creatives that provided feedback on earlier versions of the manuscript: Mary Walters, Andrew Klein, Steven Leyva, mychael zulauf, Key Bird, Randolph Bird.

Cari, Ashley, Regina, Michael Tager, Cija Jefferson, Lora Robinson, Lo Smith, Kristen, Nick, Kara, celeste doaks, Catherine, Mollye Miller, Jane Lewty. You all have been there.

The reading series and open mics in Baltimore, DC, and beyond that shaped my voice.

Running and circus communities that have been special spaces to grow when I needed movement.

The healthcare providers that saw me as a person and put me back together: Dr. Sam DuFlo, Dr. Carrie Runde, Dr. Sara Nett, Dr. Faith Reilly, and Hyeon Jin Kwon.

University of Baltimore and Rutgers, the State University of New Jersey, professors that showed me how to find my way.

My family, for your support even when you didn't quite understand the path.

My love, Jeremy.

If I missed someone: I wish I could spend another decade updating & correcting this list.

ABOUT THE AUTHOR

TRACY DIMOND is a 2016 Baker Artist Award finalist. She is the author of the full-length poetry collection, *Emotion Industry* (Barrelhouse), and four chapbooks, including *TO TRACY LIKE / TO LIKE / LIKE* (akinoga press) and *Sorry I Wrote So Many Sad Poems Today* (Ink Press), winner of *Baltimore City Paper's* Best Chapbook. She holds her MFA in Creative Writing & Publishing Arts from the University of Baltimore. Find her online at poetsthatsweat.com.

Milton Keynes UK
Ingram Content Group UK Ltd.
UKHW020751071024
449371UK00015B/1150